CLOSE ENCOUNTERS OF THE LIFE CHANGING KIND

ALISON J ASKEW

www.newgeneration-publishing.com

New Generation Publishing

Preface

Alison Askew helped to establish The Jeel Scholarship Fund in 2020 to provide educational opportunities for Palestinian youngsters who otherwise would have no chance of furthering their education and achieving their aspirations. The beneficiaries are boarders at the Jeel al Amal Boys Home in Bethany, a remarkable establishment run by the equally remarkable Najwah Sahhar. All royalties from this book and donations received will be given in full to JSF.

A visit to Jeel al Amal is the highlight of many Holy Land pilgrimages. Here pilgrims witness Christianity in action and leave inspired by young lives transformed. Alison's collection of stories draws on her experience of numerous visits to the Holy Land and she breathes life into familiar characters. Her partnership with Najwah is a modern bible story set in the village of Bethany where once Martha and Mary hosted Jesus on the eve of Palm Sunday. The teaching of Jesus is manifested in their faith and compassion for desperately needy children, of all faiths and none.

The fund is currently sponsoring two youngsters studying for nursing degrees and another who is training to be a doctor. All of them are at universities in Palestine and on qualification are keen help their local communities.

The McCabe Educational Trust is a registered charity and manages the Jeel Scholarship Fund. For more information, look at the MET pages on the McCabe Travel website. Every penny raised goes directly to the fund as The McCabe Educational Trust makes no charge for administration.

If you would like to donate to JSF or get involved in fundraising please contact Canon Michael Glanville-Smith, Chair of the JSF committee, or Alistair McCabe, Administrator of MET.

mrglanvillesmith@gmail.com
Alistair-mccabe@outlook.com
www.mccabe-travel.co.uk

Alistair McCabe, June 2023.

CONTENTS

Tomb, One Careful, Short-term Occupant.

I Shared My Son in Law with Him.

Introduction

Jesus did things differently. He began his ministry by quoting words from the prophet Isaiah saying he had come to announce good news for the poor; release for prisoners; recovery of sight for the blind and freedom for the broken victims. He seemed to be saying the focus of his ministry would be on the neediest members of society, those on the margins, not the good, the great or even the religious. He often worked spontaneously dropping his agenda to respond to the needs of those he met. He simply met people where they were and how they were and shared with them the love of God in word and deed.

We live in a world that measures success in terms of numbers, financial security, influence and social status. We tend to describe churches as 'successful' if they have large congregations, sound finances, if there are lots of professional people who hold or have held influential roles in the community.

Jesus did things differently. He said the most important people in the Kingdom of God were not the wealthy, wise or well respected, but children. Instead of choosing for his disciples men of influence, the theologically articulate, leaders in their communities, he chose an odd assortment of men comprising fishermen and tax collectors amongst others. He associated with an unlikely mix of people: women; foreigners; sinners; the sick and those on the margins of society. He took a delight in seeking those who had been left behind by society and written off by religion and invested a huge amount of time in them.

Although Jesus was followed by crowds of people and taught them, almost all of his most significant encounters were with individuals, invariably people in need. It was when he spent quality time with people on a one to one basis, with people that were seen as having no importance and little hope that lives were changed.

There's a well-known song with the words 'Love, love changes everything.... Nothing in the world will ever be the same'. For those who encountered Jesus, who experienced his love; his forgiveness; his acceptance, everything was changed and nothing would ever be the same.

The following meditations are intended to imaginatively open up the lives and worlds of some of those people. All of them show the limitless love, compassion, mercy and forgiveness of Jesus and all of them show the dignity and respect he afforded to those whom he encountered. All of them resulted in lives transformed.

Alison J Askew, Ripon, June 2023

Our Special Son. Mark10:13 -16

I can still vividly remember the day Simon was born. My wife had endured a difficult and worrying pregnancy; we were so relieved and overjoyed when our son entered the world. I was overwhelmed with a sense of pride and happiness and couldn't hold back my tears.

I was astonished at the midwife's first words to us. They weren't 'Congratulations' but 'I'm so sorry'. Sorry? Why was she sorry, this was the happiest day of our lives? I looked with undiluted love and wonder at the vulnerable little scrap, our precious, much wanted son. But the woman continued 'You can see he's not a normal baby, he'll never lead a full life, he'll have a profound learning disability'.

I was angry with her; I wanted to ask her to leave. Why couldn't she see what I did, the most beautiful, wonderful little boy?

Of course, as he grew up it was often the same reaction.

People felt sorry for us, embarrassed in Simon's company. They were blind to the uniqueness, the preciousness of Simon. We simply loved Simon as Simon. We never compared him with other children, we never regretted the way he was. He was our son, our gift from God and we loved him with an inexpressible love. He became the centre of our lives, he made us more gentle, more caring and less self centred than we might otherwise have been.

Simon truly was a blessing to us and we always only wanted the best for him.

We'd heard of Jesus the teacher and healer, the one who revealed God's love in action, the one who it was said was the personification of love and compassion. When we'd heard on the grapevine that he was coming to a village near us we determined to go to see him, to ask him to bless Simon, for we felt this was the very best thing we could do for our son. We didn't want Jesus to heal Simon to make him a 'normal' little boy, no, we loved him as he was, we didn't want him to be changed, but we longed for Jesus to bless him.

As we got near to the place where we were told Jesus was, there were lots of other proud parents who'd had the same idea, who wanted their children to be blessed. But we couldn't actually see Jesus. We were all met by his disciples who couldn't have been less welcoming if they'd tried. With one voice we cried that we'd come to see Jesus, we'd brought our children for him to bless. But they told us to go away implying that asking Jesus to bless children was a waste of his time, that he had more important things to do.

Thank God, literally, Jesus heard what was going on and intervened. He gave his disciples a good telling off. They saw things very differently. He made his point to his followers extremely clearly. He stopped what he was doing and delayed wherever he was going and made the children the centre of his world, giving them his undivided attention. It seemed like he was saying there is nothing more important than these children.

He could have raised his hands in blessing over us all, but no, he gave individual attention to each and every child undeterred by how long this might take. He took each child in his arms, laid his hands on them and blessed them. It was a wonderful moment as we handed over little Simon to him. He took him in his arms and looked at him with such love and tenderness and blessed him.

Jesus then said words that will stay with me for as long as I live. He said anyone who wanted to enter the Kingdom of God would have to become like little children for they were the greatest in God's kingdom. I'd never heard anything like it but I knew exactly what he meant. If people became vulnerable, trusting and unconditionally loving like our little Simon how much better the world would be. It wasn't just Simon who was blessed that day, we all were.

Didn't Need to go to Specsavers.
Mark 10:46 -52

I was well known if not well loved in my hometown of Jericho; Bartimaeus, the blind beggar. I was a permanent fixture by the roadside begging for money or food. I always tried to find a busy spot where plenty of people would pass by. I hadn't always been blind and so I struggled to get used to a world without sight. The hardest thing for me was the inability to work, to earn a living, to be totally dependent on the generosity and goodwill of others. I found the whole begging thing humiliating and degrading, but what choice did I have? You'll see the origins of the phrase 'Beggars can't be choosers'.

One day as I was sitting at my pitch I heard the noise of a loud crowd. People were excitedly saying that Jesus was coming this way. When the shouts became louder I tried to shout over the general cacophony attempting to attract his attention, 'Jesus, Son of David, have pity on me'. I thought I'd failed especially when the people around me kept telling me to shut up. Didn't they understand I had to seize the moment; an opportunity like this may not present itself again. I shouted even louder, desperate to be heard by Jesus.

Jesus stopped close to me and he told those nearest to him to call me. He had stopped for me, out of all the people in the crowd it was me he had called, me to whom he was going to devote his attention. The ones who had told me to shut up now spoke with kindness and encouragement. They told me to take heart, to be encouraged, because he was calling me. A new hope and energy surged within me and I flung off my cloak and hurried to the place where I had heard Jesus' voice.

He spoke to me with the utmost respect asking me what I wanted him to do for me. When I cried out to him I asked for mercy; I didn't say what form I hoped that mercy would take. Jesus may well have thought I was asking for food or money, after all that was what I asked for every day. But no, what I really wanted was to be able to see, to be able to engage fully with the world again. Jesus simply said 'Go, your faith has cured you'. What powerful words. No sooner had he spoken them than I could see. The first thing I saw was his face, the face that exuded love and compassion. How I smiled when we looked into each other's eyes.

He told me to go, but I didn't want to go, I wanted to stay with him, to follow him, and so gingerly, as he left Jericho, I tagged onto the group of his disciples and others who were following him, hoping that I could become one of them. Before he healed me I was told he was calling me. Maybe he was just calling me to come to him, but I can't help thinking he was calling me to something else, for some other reason, calling me to be his follower and that is what I would like to be.

REFLECT

1. What is it like to lose your health or something you have always taken for granted? How easy is it to adapt to a new way of life?

2. Have you ever felt people were trying to silence you when you were seeking help? If so, what was it like?

3. Jesus asks us what we would like him to do for us. What would you like him to do for you?

4. What does it mean to you to be called by Jesus?

Talk about making a dramatic entrance. Luke 5:17 -26

I don't really like being centre stage but on that occasion, I had no choice.

I was paralysed, so as you can imagine my life was severely limited, but I was fortunate.

Unlike many ill or disabled people, I had exceptional friends who would do anything for me.

We had all heard of Jesus, the great man of God who was gaining quite a reputation as a teacher and healer and one day my friends decided to take me to him to ask him to heal me. My four friends kindly put me on a stretcher and carried me to the place where we were told Jesus was. However, we weren't the only ones with that idea. When we got to the house where he was teaching my heart sank; we couldn't get anywhere near, great crowds had come from miles away. I thought my friends would admit defeat and turn round and go home. How wrong I was. They were even more determined to get to Jesus than I was and nothing was going to put them off. They warned me to hold tight and not to give up. I could never have envisaged what happened next.

My friends clambered up onto the roof of the house with my stretcher swaying with the movement. I felt totally helpless as I dangled mid-air, but they were my friends and I trusted them. Then I made a dramatic entrance through the ceiling and into the crowded house much to the bewilderment of those in the house. Jesus was clearly impressed by their faith and determination and the fact that they wouldn't let anything get in the way of me encountering him. He then told me that my sins were forgiven. It felt like a huge burden had been lifted from me. Whilst I wasn't the most sinful person in the world there were things that I had done that filled me with shame and remorse, things for which I was unable to forgive myself. How liberating that here was someone who was able to set me free. In that moment I'd even forgotten about my paralysis, for my sins had caused me a different kind of inner paralysis, of which I'd only just become aware.

I was saddened that the religious leaders rounded on Jesus accusing him of blasphemy, saying that only God had the authority to forgive sins. They had spoiled a beautiful moment.

Jesus knew what they were thinking and as if to prove he really did have the authority to forgive sins he turned to me and told me to get up, take my bed and go home. My healing was instant. Never for a moment did I question his command. I was able to stand and walk on those legs that had been useless. I received forgiveness and healing within a matter of minutes. It doesn't get any better than that. Now I didn't mind being the centre of attention, to be more accurate I wanted Jesus to be the centre of attention. I wanted to tell everyone of the amazing things he'd done for me, and I wanted to praise God for His power at work through Jesus.

I felt I was dancing on air as I joyfully returned home carrying the stretcher that for so long had carried me.

REFLECT

1. Sometimes we are unable to do things for ourselves and have to rely on family or friends. How easy do you find this?
   Who are the people who have helped to carry you? Thank God for them.

2. Sometimes we feel unable to pray and are reliant on others to carry us in their prayers.
   Can we accept this is not as a sign of failure and simply allow others to do the praying and holding for us?

3. Who are the people you carry?

4. Do you feel you have any hidden, inner paralysis? Have you asked Jesus to set you free?

Crossing Boundaries Luke. 7: 1- 10

I've always found it rather sad that most people see the world in a very black and white way. Clear and rigid demarcations have never really made sense to me and separating people into groups which are often hostile towards one another, Jews and Romans; men and women; masters and servants, what does it all mean? At the end of the day we are all human, all made of dust. We all have hopes and fears, aspirations and disappointments, we all feel joy, pain, sorrow and regret; aren't those the things that really define us?

I'm a centurion in the Roman army, which I suppose makes me a powerful and influential man, although I don't really see myself in that way and I try not to abuse my authority. I have a servant whom I love dearly, he's like one of the family to me. This poor man became seriously ill and was on the verge of dying. I was beside myself with anxiety. People couldn't understand how emotional I was. 'He's only a servant' they said, 'You can get another, servants are two a denarii'. He wasn't only a servant to me, he wasn't someone or something that I owned; he was a fellow human being who was very dear to my heart. I would have done anything to help him.

To be truthful I don't know where I stand in terms of religion. We Romans have such a multiplicity of gods we're spoiled for choice, some are more appealing and credible than others. Personally I've never subscribed to the notion of The Emperor being a god, although of course that's off the record. There is something attractive and logical about only having one god and I have built up a good relationship with my Jewish neighbours; I've tried to learn a bit about their faith and helped them build their synagogue. I'd heard about Jesus, a good man, a Jewish teacher and healer, although I gather he wasn't too popular with some of their religious leaders. I asked my friends at the synagogue if they'd approach Jesus for me and ask him to help my servant.

I saw the man whom I took to be Jesus approaching my house with the men from the synagogue. I suddenly felt an overwhelming sense of my unworthiness; I wasn't worthy to have this great man of God coming into my house, my pagan house. I said all he needed to do was speak the word, utter a command, and my servant would be healed. I had no doubt whatsoever as to his power and goodness. I know how commands work, after all I've issued plenty of them myself. I'm under the authority of my military superiors and ultimately the emperor himself, and I have a hundred soldiers under me who obey my commands.

Apparently Jesus was amazed at my response, it seemed he wasn't used to such faith even amongst his own people which I thought was strange and sad. By the time the messengers I'd sent to Jesus had returned to my house my dear servant was well, completely restored to health. It happened just as I predicted, Jesus' word was enough. None of our gods could have done that. Isn't it strange that a Roman, a foreigner, seemed to have more faith in Jesus than his own people? It just goes to show what I always believed that so many of our barriers and divisions are manmade and meaningless. The authority and compassion of Jesus seemed to transcend barriers of race, religion and class; surely that is the way we should live.

Funeral Called Off. Luke 7: 11- 17

It was the hardest day of my life; I didn't know such depths of grief were possible. I didn't think I'd ever face anything as difficult as the death of my husband all those years ago, but that was nothing compared to this, the death of my son, my only son. He and I had been alone, together, for years, he was my life, my companion, my friend as well as my son. We shared everything and he had become the man of the household. Then suddenly, with no warning my life had been shattered, fallen apart. What would I do without him; did I even want to go on without him?

Of course my neighbours were kind, spoke words of sympathy, made sure that I wasn't left on my own but none of that could change the awful reality that I was on my own, that my son was never going to walk through the door again. I'd questioned God, tried to make sense of the tragedies of my life. Wasn't it enough to have lost my husband, why now my darling son as well? There were no answers and believe me it was hard to cling on to faith in a God of love.

As the funeral procession made its way to his burial place I felt my heart had been torn out. His body which only a few days ago had been so full of life and vigour was rigid, fragile, it looked so flimsy on the wooden frame he was being carried on. I knew there was a large crowd coming to support me, but they were just a sea of faces and the whole thing seemed unreal, a dreadful mistake, a horrific nightmare.

But then I became aware of the features of one face. It was a man I'd never seen before. He had an immense compassion and sadness etched onto his face and he seemed to have some air of authority. He stepped forward through the crowd and laid his hands on my son's bier. I wondered what he was doing. He told me not to weep. The men carrying the bier stood still wondering who he was and what he was doing. He then did a really weird thing; he spoke to my dead son. He didn't speak about him, no, he spoke to him as if the lifeless body could hear him. 'Young man, I tell you get up'. Imagine my son sitting on his bier and beginning to speak. I was utterly overwhelmed, overjoyed, mystified. How had this happened? My dead son wasn't dead anymore. Jesus, for that was the healer's name, gave my son back to me. We held each other in a long, tight, silent embrace, both of us crying uncontrollable tears of joy. I had never been so happy since the day of his birth. This was like a new birth. He had been given back to me, we were re-united.

How I praised God and how I celebrated with my neighbours when we got home. Fancy, I had thought God hadn't heard my prayers and weeping, rather he sent Jesus to show his love and compassion in action, not to mention his power over death. As you can imagine this wonderful news spread like wildfire through Nain; the funeral that was called off at the last minute. Now I spend my time telling people about Jesus who raised my son from death and also gave me my life, joy and hope back. How blessed we are, how great God is.

Now I no longer have to live in the shadows. Luke 8: 43- 48

For twelve long years I had to live in the shadows; I had to make myself invisible; to pretend I wasn't there. Of course according to the law I shouldn't have been there, I should never have left the house. I was unclean, contaminated and I would defile anyone I had come into contact with. My crime? Nothing heinous. I hadn't killed anyone, cheated anyone, lied about anyone I simply had a horrible medical condition. I suffered from a constant flow of blood. I never understood how a physical ailment could be seen as sinful, something that made a person unclean. Why should someone be punished for something that wasn't their fault and over which they had no control? My house felt like a prison; how I longed to go out, to mix with people, but no, according to the religious rules I wasn't allowed to. It was barely an existence, certainly not a life. It wasn't as if I hadn't tried. I'd spent all my money on doctors and others that I thought could help me but all to no avail. Either my condition was too complex for them, or they were charlatans; sometimes it was hard to tell. But the fact remained I was no better, only poorer.

I'd heard the saying that desperate people do desperate things. Well eventually that was me. I took the law into my own hands or rather I totally bypassed the law. I'd heard about Jesus the teacher and healer who went around doing good and showing mercy, and so, mustering up all my courage I decided to take the risk of trying to see him, somehow believing that he would help me.

Perhaps I was somewhat naïve, no doubt a consequence of my lack of engagement with the world. I nearly fell at the first hurdle. I simply hadn't expected Jesus to be surrounded by such a large crowd of people. Should I just turn around and go home accepting that my hopes simply couldn't be fulfilled? No, I was sure this was the right thing to be doing and strange as it may sound I thought it was what Jesus would want me to do too. So with an equal mixture of courage and trepidation I edged my way towards Jesus, praying that no-one would recognize me. I was convinced that his power, or rather God's power at work in him, was such that I would only have to touch his cloak to be healed. I was right. I knew instantly I'd been healed just by touching the edge of his cloak. Now I just wanted to fade into the anonymity of the crowd and make my way home to my new liberated life, giving thanks to God on the way.

Again, things didn't quite work out as I'd anticipated. My quiet exit was thwarted. I suddenly found myself the centre of attention. Jesus asked who had touched him. His disciples said anyone could have nudged into him as the crowd was so large and there was a lot of pushing and shoving. But Jesus said no, that's not what he meant. He knew someone had touched him intentionally for he felt power go out of him to do someone good. I was beside myself with fear. I'd been caught out breaking the law, I was about to be publicly humiliated and vilified. I fell at his feet throwing myself on his mercy, about to ask for forgiveness. But that wasn't his agenda, although often he did forgive people. He looked at me with love and said the most beautiful words I think I've ever heard 'Daughter, your faith has healed you, go in peace'. What an affirmation. 'Daughter' not 'Woman', he recognized me as a daughter of God not someone rejected by the purity laws.

He also seemed to be praising me for my faith in him, it was that he said that had effected my cure. I was to go in peace, no longer living a life of fear in the shadows. At peace with myself, at peace with God, what more could anyone ask for?

REFLECT

1. Have you ever been in a situation where you felt you shouldn't have been there and had to make yourself invisible? How did it feel?

2. Think about and pray for those who feel trapped and those whose homes feel like prisons.

3. Are there people we still think of as unclean, undesirable, that we don't want to encounter? What does it mean to view someone as unclean?

4. Jesus called the woman 'Daughter'. Why was this so significant for her?

5. What do you think Jesus would call you? Can you accept his description of you?

6. What does it mean to have God's peace?
   What do we mean in Holy Communion when we say 'The peace of the Lord be always with you' and 'Go in peace to love and serve the Lord'?

A Thank You Doesn't cost anything.
Luke 17:12- 19

It's strange isn't it, the things that define us and how they change when our situation alters. We all probably identify with certain groups where we feel we belong and feel other groups are alien to us, to our experiences and beliefs and we feel excluded from them. Well that was certainly true for me.

I'm a Samaritan and our religion and national identity was what defined me. That was where I belonged, that was who I was. But then totally unexpected events outside my control changed the way I saw myself and the way others saw me.

To begin with like so many others in my position I was in denial. At first I put the dropping of things down to clumsiness or lack of concentration, the loss of movement in my hands down to something else. Then the telltale signs became more obvious; I couldn't ignore them any longer and other people were looking at me and commenting. The dreadful truth was that I had leprosy. Our community is a small, tightknit one, we look after each other, but as soon as my family and neighbours knew that I was afflicted with this dreaded disease they couldn't get rid of me quickly enough. I was banished, became an outcast, unwanted, encouraged to move as far away as possible. I was no longer a Samaritan, I was a leper.

I didn't know any lepers; I don't suppose anyone does until they become one. So driven out by family and friends I found a new community who like me were lepers, feared and unwelcome. Our illness became our new identity, it was the thing that bound us together. Whatever the differences in our beliefs and backgrounds these things became irrelevant, the bond of leprosy was much stronger and was what set us apart from others. We travelled around together keeping away from centres of population and warning others of our approach. Initially I would have been seen as an outsider, a foreigner, an enemy amongst the others who were all Jews, but now that no longer mattered. In the face of our shared leprosy, our old religious and nationalistic identity paled into insignificance. We were doomed men; the walking, or rather shuffling dead.

My nine companions, my new brothers, being Jewish, had heard of Jesus who apparently was a Jewish healer and wonderworker, someone who took pity on helpless cases like us and those whom society had rejected. We encountered Jesus on the outskirts of a village between Galilee and Samaria. Of course we couldn't come close to him but my friends called out to him at the top of their voices 'Jesus, master, take pity on us'. I wasn't sure if I should be asking him for anything as I didn't belong to his religion or really have any claims on his time or sympathy. He told us to go and show ourselves to the priests. That seemed a curious and very premature thing to be asked to do. According to the Jewish law people showed themselves to a priest when they'd been healed of leprosy and the priest was the one who confirmed the cure and pronounced that they were now fit to return to their community and normal life. I didn't quite get what was going on but encouraged by my friends, I set off on the journey to the priest. Whilst we were on our way we all noticed the same extraordinary thing: the sensation had come back into our hands, the dry flakey skin had disappeared and been replaced by new healthy skin and our legs had lost the pain and regained strength.

We laughed and cried for joy, we hugged each other and with our new healed bodies ran all the way to the priest knowing Jesus had healed us and given us our lives back. The priest merely confirmed what we already knew, we were well, we were no longer lepers. He looked at each one of us in turn and made his pronouncement that we could go home, be re-united with family and friends and re-enter society. I was the last one to be seen, waiting to hear those liberating words. I was overwhelmed with emotion so much so that I hadn't noticed my erstwhile brothers had all left and were making their way home as soon as they could. My joy at being healed was tinged with a little sadness that they hadn't even stopped to say 'Goodbye' or to wish me well. But then, we were no longer lepers, the close bond that had united us had now been broken.

I couldn't wait to get home to see my family and friends after all this time, but yes, I could wait, I must wait, there was something even more important to do first. I had an overwhelming desire to go back to thank Jesus for what he had done for me. Perhaps that was where the other nine had rushed off with such speed. When I found Jesus I felt lost for words, 'Thank you' seemed so inadequate. I fell at his feet and blurted out my inexpressible gratitude. He seemed genuinely pleased to see me, it was the conclusion to my healing, an acknowledgement that it was all down to him. The other nine? I never saw them again and nor did he. How sad that they couldn't find a few minutes to thank the man who'd given them back the whole of their lives.

Now I'm healed and welcomed back into my own community I'm committed to being part of a new, wider community, the community of the grateful and thankful, the community that regardless of religious affiliation remembers to give thanks to God.

REFLECT

1. What groups do you identify with? Where do you feel you belong? Has your sense of identification changed throughout your life?

2. It's easy to ask God for help, do we find it as easy to say Thank You when we receive that help? How prominent is thanksgiving in your prayer life?

3. Do we make time to thank those who help and support us?

4. Are our churches thankful communities?

The Day of the Tax Cuts in Jericho.
Luke 19:1-10

I wasn't one of life's good guys, in fact I was the most hated man in town.

When people saw me they would shout out insults or obscenities. Some would even spit at me.

You see I was a tax collector. Tax collectors have never been popular anywhere in the world, and I don't suppose they ever will be, but in my case it was worse. I was a cheating tax collector; I charged people more than they owed and there wasn't much they could do about it. Even worse than that, I was a traitor to my own people. I was a Jew working for the Romans, the hated occupying force who made our lives a misery and had no respect for our religion and sacred laws; the Romans who called their emperor a god and made us use coins bearing his image.

Yes, I was hated and despised, and rightly so. I was also what these days you'd call vertically challenged: I was very short.

I suppose I'd become increasingly uncomfortable with my lifestyle, or had I just got too old to cope with the daily barrage of insults, knowing I was hated wherever I went? Perhaps it was a bit of both. Anyhow, when I heard that Jesus was coming to our town, Jericho, I was determined to see him, and for him to see me. But that was the challenge. There was a crowd and as I said, I'm short, a good six inches shorter than most men. I'd never see him over the crowd of people that had gathered.

There was only one thing for it. I decided to climb the nearest sycamore tree where I'd have a bird's eye view. I swallowed my pride because I was desperate. Of course the crowd reveled in the sight. 'Look at shorty up a tree, the cheat is there for all to see'. I could put up with their laughter and name calling so long as I saw Jesus; that was all that mattered.

My plan worked. As Jesus approached he saw me perched up in the tree full of anticipation. To be fair, it would have been hard for him not to have seen me; after all, grown men don't sit in trees, that's what kids do. The ridiculing crowd did me a favour too. If somehow Jesus hadn't seen me, he couldn't have missed the commotion and hostility at the bottom of the tree and would have looked up to see its cause.

Then the most amazing thing happened: he looked up at me and called me down. It flashed through my mind that no-one had ever looked up at me: they always looked down at me and looked down on me. This was a new experience. He called me by my name, not 'cheat', 'traitor' or 'shorty' or the other names I was usually called, but my own name Zacchaeus, the name I'd probably never been called in all of my adult life. As I climbed down from the tree my feelings of worthlessness began to fall away like a snake shedding its skin. I was someone; I was Zacchaeus.

As I was coming to terms with this new reality something even more amazing happened. Jesus invited himself to my house for a meal. I can't remember the last time anyone came to my house; people would avoid it like a plague house as if by crossing the threshold they would become contaminated. But Jesus wanted to come, he took the initiative. How extraordinary. I couldn't believe it, nor could the crowd. 'What, he's going to the home of the cheating, sinful tax collector?' I could understand their horror and anger. After all there were plenty of good, religious, law abiding people in Jericho, why had he chosen to come to my home and not theirs? I set off with a skip in my step like a happy, carefree child as I led Jesus to my house.

Jesus was so gracious and merciful, he showed me such love. He didn't criticise me or make me feel bad; in truth, I had never felt so good about myself. He didn't tell me how to make amends for my previous greedy, cheating lifestyle, I already knew. I promised him I would more than repay those whom I had cheated and I would never cheat or overcharge anyone again. They weren't idle promises, I kept my word.

The wonderful thing was Jesus changing my life had a knock on effect for everyone in Jericho. He had changed my life and I was able to change theirs'. From that day on there was no more cheating, no-one paid more than they owed. I looked out for those who were poor and struggling financially and discreetly tried to help them. I didn't do it to become popular; I did it because it was the right thing to do, and I know it's what he would have done. He had a special place in his heart for the poor as he had for sinners, folk like me. Like I said, I wasn't trying to become popular or receive praise but from then on I was never called names, I was no longer ignored in the street. People would come to speak to me, to ask me how I was. I had become a normal member of the community; I had been forgiven and re-habilitated.

Climbing that tree was the best thing I ever did. Jesus gave me a new start in life and the lives of everyone in Jericho were blessed. I think the story of the cheating tax collector who became a good guy will be told for many years to come.

REFLECT

1. Who are the people who are looked down on and despised in our society?
    Is this judgement deserved?

2. Do you feel that for whatever reason people have sometimes looked down on you?
    How does it feel to know that Jesus never does this?

3. What does it mean to be seen by Jesus?

4. How does it feel to know that Jesus calls you by name, that he sees you as an individual and loves you for who you are not what you might become?

5. How do you respond to God's love, welcome and forgiveness?

What's in a name?
Luke 23:13 -25, John 18:28- 19:16

Names are powerful things, much more than just labels.

They define us; they help shape the people we become.

Many parents give their children aspirational names suggesting what they'd like them to become or the qualities they'd like them to have.

It didn't work like that for me.

Barabbas, son of a father, in other words no-one knew the name or identity of my father.

You could say my name means the illegitimate one,

Or putting it colloquially, 'Bastard'.

What a name to be known by! No aspiration there. Did my name shape the person I became?

My mother had a constant stream of lovers, often more than one at a time, or so I'm told. All of them were bad apples, on the wrong side of the law, most of them one night stands; none of them wanting a sense of commitment or family life. My mother told me she honestly had no idea who my father was, he could have been one of several. She loved me, but she was weak, she spoiled me perhaps because she felt guilty that I had no father. That meant I had no male role model, no-one to set boundaries or impose discipline. I quickly got into trouble. I became an angry young man: angry at my circumstances, angry at my lack of opportunities, angry at society, angry with the occupying Romans and angry with God. My anger got played out in random acts of violence and crime.

As I grew older my anger and frustration became more focused, I came to realise I could make a name for myself as a rebel against Rome. I could become somebody by being the leader of riots and insurrections. I could shape an identity, I could gain respect from those who wanted our country to be free from the scourge of the occupying Romans. I could use violence. I could kill in a just cause. Of course it was a risky course of action, I knew if I was identified as the ring leader, if I was caught there would be a heavy price to pay, perhaps I would have to pay with my life, but there would be a glory in dying a martyr.

Eventually the inevitable happened. I was arrested for causing a riot and committing a murder. I was brought before Pontius Pilate the Roman governor and was awaiting my certain death sentence. I couldn't appeal against it, it was cut and dried, there was no question I was guilty. But it was my lucky day.

There was a great commotion in Pilate's headquarters surrounding another man who'd been arrested on what seemed to me fairly dubious charges of blasphemy, claiming to be a king and leading a rebellion against Rome. I couldn't believe my eyes - he was the least likely looking rebel possible - meek, submissive, blood stained and battered. He seemed to make no reply to all the charges brought against him however outlandish they sounded.

The crowd egged on by our religious leaders clearly hated him and wanted him out of the way. Their angry cries demanded his crucifixion. Clearly, they would be satisfied with nothing less.

Pilate wasn't a man known for his compassion or leniency but even he baulked against this. He wanted to set Jesus free with a warning but was afraid of the reaction of the hostile crowd. Pilate reminded them that they had a custom that at Passover they were entitled to have a prisoner released, did they want him to release Jesus? Well that was red rag to a bull. Their response was deafening and unanimous 'No, not him but Barabbas'.

I couldn't believe my ears, I never expected this turn of events. I'm not a man known for having any moral code but even I could see this was all wrong. I was a murderer, a leader of rebellion and I was being freed, but Jesus who had done nothing wrong was clearly being framed and led out to his death. He died in my place.

I had heard about him before, how he healed the sick, forgave people of their sins, showed God's love and compassion but called into question some of the rigid and oppressive religious rules. He sounded like a thoroughly good bloke. I also remembered he had called God his father, he had taught his followers to pray to God as Abba, Father; he claimed to be the son of The Father. Unlike me he knew his identity, he was clear of his origins. Son of The Father meet son of a father! But it was the true son who was killed and the bastard son who was allowed to live.

That day marked a new start for me: the first day of the rest of my life. I decided to leave behind my old violent, angry way of life and to live differently. Seeing him, the Son of The Father being led away to execution I realised I too could be a son of The Father. Like so many others whose lives had been touched by him I realised I was loved, forgiven and valued by my Father in Heaven. I had a new identity and for the first time in my life I felt I mattered.

I wish he could have lived to see the change his death brought about in me.

What a Party! John 2:1 -11

Although I say it myself, we put on a good wedding here in Cana, Galilee. Of course hospitality is at the very heart of our culture; we love to offer food and drink to others, to celebrate together. Perhaps subconsciously it's a mirroring of the generosity and hospitality we receive from God.

I'm well known in this town, my family has lived here for as long as anyone can remember and that means I know everyone, their families, their histories, and their stories. Because I'm trusted I'm often asked to act as wine steward at weddings and other big occasions in the community. It's an honour but it's also quite a responsibility. The art is ensuring that everyone has enough wine to have a good time and enter fully into the joy of the occasion but being careful nobody has too much so that they become loud and unpleasant. There are always the odd few that push their luck and have to be taken in hand.

Well, the particular wedding in question will always play a part in the history of our town. I thought it was going to end in disaster but in fact quite the reverse proved to be the case; it was a triumph. I was beginning to get a bad feeling that something wasn't quite right. I could see Mary, a lovely lady whom I know well and respect, talking to her son Jesus. It soon became apparent there wasn't enough wine for the remainder of the feast. A terrible panic arose within me, what would we do, how could we save the occasion? There would be a riot; my reputation would be in tatters, but more importantly what should have been the happiest day in the young couple's life was about to end in shame and disgrace. It wasn't my fault, I hadn't ordered the wine, I wasn't actually in charge of the catering, that was someone higher up the chain, the master of the feast. None the less I was the chief wine steward with others working for me, I had my pride and my personal involvement with this couple whom I'd known since they were children.

Somehow, somewhere along the line things had gone badly wrong. Either insufficient wine had been bought or a large number of people had gatecrashed the occasion. Either way it didn't really matter, the end result was the same – too many people and too little wine, disaster. As I sank into an abyss of despair and shame Mary came to me quietly but authoritatively 'Do whatever Jesus tells you', those were her words. As far as I knew Jesus was a teacher and ex carpenter and a number of his friends were fishermen. What possible expertise did they have in wedding feasts?

In the hall where the feast was being held were six huge water jars, the kind we use for religious washing and purification. I guess each one would have held about twenty five gallons. Jesus' 'plan' was that my colleagues and I filled these jars with water. Naturally I was incredulous. It was wine we needed not water. I knew Jesus was a good man and that he clearly wanted to help and make things right but really, what good would a hundred and fifty gallons of water be unless everyone had suddenly become teetotal? If you've ever tried moving or carrying water you'll know how heavy it is. Anyone who has ever tried to bale water out of a sinking ship will vouch for that. How long was it going to take to fill those vast jars? I didn't understand what we were doing or what purpose it would serve but at least it was a distraction, something to do.

When we'd finished Jesus told me to draw off some of the water and take it to the master of the feast. Everything in me wanted to protest. What in the world could I say as I presented the master of ceremonies with the meagre, insulting offering of a cup of water? I wanted to disappear into a hole in the ground, to wake up and find the whole thing had been a disturbing nightmare. But ridiculous as Jesus' instruction was he spoke it with authority and conviction, and so going against all my reason and common sense I did what he said.

I was expecting criticism and humiliation, instead I received praise and admiration on the quality of the wine I had given him, for somehow between me drawing off the water and the master of the feast tasting it, it had been transformed into wine. Not just any old wine mind you, but wine of the very highest quality. I can't explain it but I know it happened because I was involved. In the course of a few minutes we'd gone from no wine to more wine than the guests could possibly drink, and no-one apart from Mary, Jesus and I was any the wiser as to what had happened.

My initial thoughts were those of profound relief. None of the guests, the master of the feast or the couple themselves had any idea that we'd run out of wine. All embarrassment, humiliation and recrimination had been avoided and everyone had a good time celebrating the love of the young couple for the remainder of the feast.

But as I mulled it over I thought there was more to it than this. Yes, Jesus had acted out of compassion, out of a concern for the couple, their family and guests but that only seemed to be part of what had happened. He didn't need to have provided so much wine and such good quality wine, far better than what we'd started off with. It seemed to be about unexpected generosity, even prodigality, all given in a very understated, anonymous way. It was only later when I explained what had happened that people knew what Jesus had done. I think we all have a lot of talking and thinking to do to really understand the message Jesus was trying to give us. There seem to be so many layers of meaning; a bit like savouring and appreciating a really good wine.

No more queuing. John 5: 1-15

I don't like complaining or wallowing in self-pity but often I thought life was a bit of a bummer, that is until I met Jesus.

You see I was lame, had been for thirty eight years. That's an awfully long time, longer than many people's life time. To begin with I hoped and prayed that one day I'd wake up and I could walk; of course that never happened. I'd tried exercising, stretching, positive thinking but all to no avail. In the early days I went to see doctors but all that did was use up the few savings I had and none of them could help me. It really felt like a life sentence. After a few years the friends and relatives who had been happy to help me gradually disappeared and I can't blame them. I had become a burden and wasn't cheerful company. And so for as long as I can remember I shuffled my way to the Sheep Pool here in Jerusalem, often I just lay there for days at a time. I felt the pool was my last chance, my best hope. The pool was well known for its curative properties. Periodically the waters of the pool stirred, some believed this was caused by an angel, and when the waters moved, the first person to enter them was cured. I suppose all's fair in love and disability. There was no such thing as an orderly queue or a recognition of who had been there the longest or whose need was the greatest. Ironically it was those who were least disabled who got there first as they were fit enough to be the first into the water. Those who had friends or relatives with them did well too as they got the help they needed to get into the pool when the waters had stirred.

You might ask why I even bothered staying there as it never worked for me, but actually what alternatives did I have? At least some of those who came to the pool gave me food to keep body and soul together and on a cold night some even lent me a blanket. Pathetic as it sounds there was also company, people to talk to. Like I said, I'd lost touch with my family and friends long ago. This odd assortment of ill people and their friends became my only companions. My life had been reduced to one of begging and dependency as well as immobility.

Then one day everything changed. A man who I'd never seen before appeared at the pool. He had a rare gift of intuition and out of all the people waiting and longing at the pool his attention was drawn to me. It was if he knew my circumstances without anyone having told him. This man, Jesus, asked me if I wanted to be made well. You might think that was a pretty stupid and insulting question to ask, but it was the right question. After all those years of being paralysed it was the only life I knew, did I really want to begin a new life where I'd have to take responsibility for myself, where I could no longer beg and rely on the charity of others? It was a real question but I knew the answer was 'Yes' I did want to be healed and I was prepared to take on my new responsibilities should I be healed. I explained to Jesus that it wasn't for lack of desire or motivation but I simply couldn't get to the pool in time to be cured and I had no-one to help me. I wasn't playing the sympathy card that was just how things were.

Jesus looked me in the eye and gave me a very direct instruction 'Stand up, take your mat and walk'. Something about him just made me do it in spite of how ridiculous the words sounded. You might have thought if I was capable of doing that I'd have done it long ago, but no, now was the right time. My healing was instant and I was able to walk, taking my mat with me.

Rather than being congratulated on my healing I was apprehended by the Pharisees, the religious men who were so keen on upholding the minutiae of the religious laws. 'It's the Sabbath' they said, ' what are you doing working by carrying your mat?' It had never really struck me before how petty and limiting some of the laws were. I had just been healed after thirty-eight years; did God really want me to wait until the next day to celebrate my healing?

REFLECT

1. 'It's not fair' is a common complaint and the reality is life isn't fair. There is a great inequality and disparity between rich and poor nations. Even in our own country there is huge inequality between the richest and poorest and people living in different areas. Often the people in greatest need are voiceless and have few champions.
What groups do you think are most disadvantaged and disenfranchised?

2. What can we do to highlight their needs?

3. Are local churches attentive and responsive to the needs of those in their communities?

4. What responsibilities come with being well?

5. Pray for those who feel that they are always at the back of the queue in life.

Now I've got a story to tell. John 6: 1-13

My name is Joe. I'm a very ordinary, some would say boring, young lad from Galilee.

The other local boys and my classmates always seemed to have tales to tell of their exploits and adventures. I was envious when I heard of the hills they'd climbed; the huge fish they'd caught; the hikes they'd been on and of course I was all too aware of their successes at school.

I didn't seem to have any particular gift, I wasn't academic or sporty, I wasn't artistic, I was always in the background, I never had anything exciting to tell my friends. I guess part of the problem is I'm shy and rather lacking in confidence. I'm an only child and some say I'm a Mummy's boy. My mum and I have a very close relationship and perhaps she is a bit over protective of me.

Anyhow, the other day something amazing happened, something that changed my life. Now everyone wants to be my friend and hear my story. I've suddenly become a bit of a hero.

My Aunt, my Mum's sister, had heard about Jesus the itinerant preacher who'd got quite a reputation as a healer, and when she knew he was going to be in the area she wanted to go and see him for herself. I asked my Mum if I could go too and as I was going to be with my Aunt and older cousins my Mum felt I couldn't come to any harm and said I could go.

After a bit of a walk we came to a place that was so green, the grass was like a carpet and so we sat down next to other groups of families and friends. I didn't really know what to expect. Was I going to be bored listening to a long religious lesson? It didn't feel like it was going to be boring though. More and more people kept arriving, I've never seen such a crowd; they were obviously expecting something. There was a real buzz and a great sense of excitement.

I wasn't sure what I expected Jesus to look like but when I caught a glimpse of him, he was just an ordinary man, no fancy clothes, no superhero aura, just like anyone's dad, brother or cousin from our area.

Jesus was up on the hillside with his followers and they were deep in conversation. The next thing I knew one of them who said his name was Andrew came up to me. He asked if I'd hand over my picnic lunch to him so he could give it to Jesus. My Mum had sent me out with a very generous lunch, five barley loaves and two fishes, I don't know how she thought I was going to eat it all although perhaps she didn't know how long I'd be out for, or maybe she thought I could share it with my cousins if they'd forgotten to bring their own food. I never thought twice about it, I simply handed over my lunch. I got a look of disapproval and disbelief from my cousins - clearly they hadn't brought any food of their own and weren't best pleased that I'd given mine away as they were hoping to share it. As I looked around I could see that no-one apart from me seemed to have brought food. How strange, going out for the day into the middle of nowhere and not taking anything to eat.

I certainly wasn't expecting what happened next, I don't suppose anyone was.

Jesus took my lunch and held it up in prayer thanking God for it, then with the disciples' help he started to hand it out to everyone in the crowd. How did he do it? It was truly a miracle. I've never been much good at maths, but even I could work out that five loaves and two fishes can't feed five thousand people, but somehow they did. I looked as far as the eye could see and everyone was eating. What a picnic! Jesus didn't tell people they should have brought their own food and they should have been better prepared, it seemed like he just wanted to do something generous and lovely for us all. I thought maybe that is what God is like, giving people more than they deserve or even thought of asking for. I knew I'd never read the scriptures in the same way again, this meal had brought them to life in a new way.

When we'd all had plenty to eat Jesus got his disciples to collect the food that was left so that none of it was wasted. Can you believe it; out of my picnic lunch there were twelve baskets of scraps left over after five thousand people were fed. It's mind blowing isn't it! I wish my Mum had been here to see it. If I hadn't been there myself I simply wouldn't have believed it.

Jesus is absolutely amazing. I hope I get another chance to see him. It makes me feel so special that I played a little part in that fantastic miracle. I wonder what would have happened if I'd hidden my lunch and hadn't handed it over to Jesus? Maybe that's the point, Jesus needs us to work with him and hand over to him what we have so he can do wonderful things with it.

Rescued from Death Row and given another chance. John 8:1-11

He said he loved me; he pleaded with me to be his lover, promised he'd protect me and safeguard my reputation. How stupid I was, how gullible to be taken in by his words.

When the over-zealous religious law enforcers, the Temple morality police arrived at his house and found us in bed it was a different story. Suddenly I had become the instigator of the illicit relationship. Allegedly I had enticed him into bed; it was all my fault.

Of course, he didn't stand by me when the religious voyeurs and law enforcers arrived.

How I despised those men who delighted in the weaknesses and shortcomings of others as if they were morally perfect themselves. Imagine, getting a kick out of spying on people's private lives, delighting in their secret sins and failings and longing to report those misdeeds to the religious authorities. Of course it was mainly women they shopped, but anyone who broke the Sabbath laws for whatever reason, or failed to keep the rules surrounding ritual cleanliness was fair game as well. The laws themselves sickened me.

They weren't God's laws; they were man made. They bore all the hallmarks of male domination, control and a total lack of compassion. Why was a woman when she was menstruating or had given birth, both perfectly natural occurrences, regarded as unclean? Why wasn't it possible to walk on the Sabbath to visit a sick relative? Surely these couldn't be the rules of a loving, merciful God.

But back to my story. When those self-righteous men arrived at my lover's door my heart sank. I knew the penalty under 'God's Law'; adultery meant death by stoning. They dragged me out of the house not sparing my blushes and took me to a preacher who'd been making quite a name for himself, Jesus from Nazareth. It was at that point that my fortunes changed. He clearly wasn't the typical rabbi or religious leader who stuck rigidly to the letter of the law oblivious to the spirit behind it. I was waiting for his disapproving stare and words of condemnation as he heard the charge against me. He didn't tell them not to hurl stones at me and give me my just deserts he simply said to them that the person who was without sin should take the first shot.

I waited in trepidation for the sinless one to start the process, looking at the hardened expressions of my accusers. But there was an embarrassed silence. The men started looking at one another and then slowly and silently they began to walk away hanging their heads. They had failed in their mission and had been humiliated. As well as saving my life, Jesus had done something profound. He had got those puritanical, critical religious men to realise that they too were sinful and had no right to point the finger or hurl the stone at others. I was utterly amazed and slowly realised I wasn't going to die.

I had heard people talking about Jesus saying he was sinless, so by his own judgement he had the right to cast the first, and it seemed only stone. But he didn't. He asked me if anyone had condemned me and when I said 'No-one' he said neither did he condemn me but he added 'From this moment do not sin again'.

It was a new start for me. I could choose to live differently, to try to live a good, sinless life but I could also learn to look at myself with compassion knowing that I had been forgiven and would be forgiven again, for Jesus had shown me that God is full of love and mercy, that He operates according to an economy of grace and not of law. What a strange thing: if I hadn't been caught committing adultery I'd never have discovered the true nature of God as revealed in Jesus.

REFLECT

1. Do you think the church, or certain parts of it, has a tendency to be too critical of the shortcomings of others? What about you?

2. Do you think the church is over obsessed about matters of sexual impropriety at the expense of more important failings?

3. Sometimes churches and Christians are so concerned with keeping the letter of the law that they lose sight of the spirit of it. How can we guard against this?

4. God forgives us; can we forgive ourselves and others?

5. How does God's forgiveness lead us to a new start?

Strange Reactions. John 9:1-41

I never cease to be amazed by people's reactions, and being blind you tend to be more tuned in to what you hear and what you sense; you pick up vibes.

I was born blind, I don't know why, sometimes these things just happen. I never really asked 'Why?' it was just how things were. Of course my blindness affected everything. When I was younger it must have put an enormous strain on my parents and as I grew older it meant I couldn't take part in the normal activities of life, I was always rather on the margins.

Unlike people who become blind I'd never known what it was like to see and I never expected to be able to see, but Jesus changed all of that.

One day I heard people talking about me asking why I'd been born blind; whose fault was it, mine or my parents'? That question made me angry. What a stupid and simplistic equation; as if someone's sin caused blindness. If I was born blind I hadn't had any chance to sin, and my parents are good people, I can't believe that their sins caused them to have a blind son. Then the man that I later realised was Jesus confirmed my belief, that simply isn't how things work. He talked about light and doing the works of God; that sounded much more constructive. I've always liked to look for the positive rather than the negative. Jesus said he was the light of the world. That was an image full of hope and promise.

But he wasn't just all words, his words became translated into actions. He made a sticky potion of mud and saliva and rubbed it onto my eyes and then told me to go to the pool of Siloam and wash. I didn't ask 'Why?' or question what was the point of the strange instruction, I just did it. That simple little action resulted in me being able to see for the first time ever. That's quite a thing. Suddenly the world had opened up in a new way for me. So much to take in – colours; shapes; textures; sizes but most wondrous of all the faces of those people I'd known and heard all my life but had never seen. I was utterly overjoyed and amazed, but strangely not everyone else reacted in the same way.

Some people who knew me well even questioned my identity saying I wasn't the man who'd been the blind beggar I just looked like him. Forgive the pun but that beggars belief. I told them plainly 'It's me; I am the man that was the blind beggar'. Isn't it strange that when something wonderful, something out of the ordinary happens, people will look for any explanation other than the truth.

The religious leaders were like a dog with a bone; they wouldn't give up and refused to accept that Jesus had healed me. They tried to turn something good into something bad saying whoever Jesus was he couldn't be from God as he didn't observe the Sabbath. Although not a religious expert I felt confident to remonstrate with them, if Jesus was a sinner how could he have cured me? They asked me what I had to say about him and I replied that he was a prophet.

I wasn't quite sure that was the right word but I wanted them to know I was sure he was sent by God. They wouldn't take my word for it and sent for my parents to verify that I was their son and had been born blind. What extraordinary scepticism. What reason had I to invent the account of what had happened?

Like I've said, my parents are good people but I could tell they felt intimidated by the religious leaders. It was almost as if they were being accused of something. They were subjected to a barrage of hostile questions: Is he your son? Was he born blind? How is it he can now see? I don't blame them, they tried to step back, to get out of the firing line. Of course they vouched for the fact that that I was their son and had been born blind but they said they didn't know how I could now see or who had opened my eyes. Surely I was best placed to answer those questions, after all I was an adult according to Jewish law.

For holy men I found them disappointing and vindictive. They seemed to be afraid of Jesus' power and goodness. I remember thinking heaven help us if they are the religious experts, the ones we should listen to and respect; they were so blind to the truth. It takes an ex-blind man to recognize blind men. They actually accused him of being a sinner. I was emboldened by their lies and scheming. 'Listen' I said, 'I was blind but now I see; that's the simple truth'. Sometimes speaking in a simple, direct way is the most powerful form of communication. I realised they wouldn't listen to any explanations or interpretations I might have offered; they had written their script and were not prepared to listen to any alternatives.

I was so incensed by their obvious hatred of Jesus that I didn't hold back, I was prepared to take them on for the sake of the truth. I don't know where my courage came from, perhaps it was another gift from God. I taunted them asking if they wanted to become Jesus' disciples, knowing this was the last thing on their minds. They proudly said they were disciples of Moses and as if a condemnation said I was the one that was Jesus' disciple. They questioned Jesus' origins and background saying they didn't know where he was from. In other words, he was an unknown, he didn't fit into their inflexible, regimented schema. I pointed out the obvious which even a child would have seen. How amazing, you don't know where he's from and yet he opened my eyes; he has done what no-one else has ever done, surely God wouldn't listen to him if he was a sinner. Clearly they couldn't cope with that challenge, that truth, and accused me of having been born in sin and so having no understanding of the things of God, and they drove me away. So much for love and kindness.

But that wasn't the end of the story, Jesus came looking for me. He asked me if I believed in The Son of Man and I asked who the Son of Man was so that I could believe in him. I should have guessed, it was Jesus. I was all too happy to profess my unquestioning belief and offer him my worship.

Jesus then said something extraordinary, but actually what I had begun to work out for myself, that he had come into the world to help people see, to open their eyes to the love, mercy and generosity of God and to point out the blindness of those who think they can see but claim a monopoly on understanding the ways of God.

Sight is so much more than just seeing the physical. Thanks to Jesus I not only received my physical sight but became able to see and perceive the things of God in a new and fresh way. I think the second is the even greater miracle.

I feel sorry for the religious leaders that they are not even prepared to open their eyes to the possibility of new insights. I pray that they too will be healed and receive their sight.

REFLECT

1. Do you believe that God causes illnesses or disabilities as a punishment for sin?
   How do you think this belief arose?

2. How important is the image of light to you?

3. Do you think that seeing is more than having physical sight?
   Has your ability to see, to perceive things changed over the years, if so, how?

4. Do you know people who refuse to see, who won't accept anything that challenges their world view?
   In what ways is the church sometimes blind?

5. What new insights has God given to you? How have they enriched your life?

He was like one of the Family.
Luke 10:38 -42, John 11:1 -53, John 12: 1 -11

It's hard to know where to start when talking about Jesus; he meant so much to us, my sister Mary, my brother Lazarus and me, Martha. He changed all of our lives. It was a great privilege that Jesus saw us as friends and chose to use our home in Bethany as a stopping off place when he was on his way to Jerusalem as we were just over the top of the Mount of Olives. Life must have been very demanding for him; everyone wanting a bit of him, asking him questions, seeking his help, it must have been hard to find time just to rest and unwind, to escape from the needs of others for a while. I think that's what we were able to provide for him. He constantly gave so much of himself to others it was gratifying to think that in some small way we could give something to him. He used to say that when he came to our home he felt he could just relax and as it were put his feet up. He became like one of the family. We laughed and joked together and simply enjoyed each other's company. Of course Jesus never talked about other people but he did sometimes say how tired he felt or how frustrated he was when people misunderstood him or twisted his words.

When I knew he was coming I always made a big effort to ensure that the house was tidy and that he would have a good nourishing meal; that's the kind of thing I'm good at. I wanted to be the perfect hostess to show him how much I appreciated his visits. I remember on one occasion I got quite cross with Jesus and told him so because I didn't think he appreciated all the effort I'd gone to while Mary did nothing but just sat at his feet and listened to him. For someone who devoted his life to the service of others I thought he'd have taken my side.....When I voiced my frustration that Mary hadn't lifted a finger to help with the meal but was just sitting listening to him he said I was fussing about lots of things but Mary had chosen the better path. Charming I thought: if we'd both sat at his feet there'd have been no food. On reflection I think I saw what he meant. Sometimes we can be so busy doing things that we don't make time or space to listen to what God may want to say to us. Jesus' teaching was his gift to us and I thought I was too busy to value his gift. I think he wanted me to know that perhaps I needed to slow down and not fill every moment with activity and busyness. But he loved us both and I think he could appreciate that we did things differently and showed our love for him in different ways.

It's hard to put into words the extraordinary thing Jesus did for our brother Lazarus. How many people can claim their brother was raised from the dead and called out of his tomb still wearing his grave clothes? But initially it was another occasion when I vented my frustration at Jesus. Of course it was rather irrational, but I felt if he'd got to our house earlier Lazarus wouldn't have died. It's always easy to blame someone else isn't it? I knew Jesus would just take it on the chin.

Jesus told me Lazarus would rise again, I said I knew that, at the resurrection on the last day, but frankly that was of little comfort in the here and now. Then he spoke to me those incredible words 'I am the resurrection and the life, whoever has faith in me shall live even though he dies'.

I suddenly realised who he was: he wasn't just our friend Jesus, he wasn't simply a wise teacher, no, I was in the very presence of The Messiah, God's own son. For once it was me and not Mary who was listening to him, hanging on his every word. Jesus was God's own son and yet how powerful were his human emotions too. He wept from the very depth of his being when we took him to our brother's tomb. Was he weeping for us, for Lazarus, for the human condition or perhaps for himself? Who knows, but we could see without any shadow of a doubt how much he loved us all. What power he exuded as he cried out to our dead brother in his tomb to come out. It was almost comical to see our recently buried brother shuffle out of his tomb still enclosed in his burial clothes. Jesus told us to loose him, to set him free.

What a tragedy and irony that Lazarus' raising from the dead became the cause of a concerted campaign to kill Jesus. I know Jesus wouldn't have wanted us to feel guilty about the effect his kindness and generosity to us had on his own safety, and indeed survival, but it was hard not to feel a level of responsibility for him when the religious authorities were looking for a way to kill him because of Lazarus.

I think our sense of foreboding about Jesus' safety led Mary to do what some criticized and some felt was highly controversial. But she knew what she was doing and why she was doing it and she didn't really care what other people thought. Just before Passover we decided to have a special supper in Jesus' honour. As usual I served, which I was very happy to do. Mary brought out a pound of very expensive perfume, oil of pure nard, and anointed Jesus' feet with it and wiped them with her hair. What a beautiful gesture of love and generosity. There was a gorgeous, heady smell permeating the house, it was like a fragrant offering rising up to God. Judas Iscariot, who shortly after proved to be Jesus' betrayer, was highly critical of what Mary had done saying her action was wasteful and the perfume could have been used much more profitably by being sold and the proceeds given to the poor. He had completely missed the point of what Mary had done and why she'd done it. Jesus said 'Let her keep it for the day of my burial'. I think thoughts of his impending death were on his mind. All that would come soon enough but for now we simply wanted to celebrate his presence with us and rejoice in his love and friendship and show our gratitude for the way in which he had changed all of our lives.

REFLECT

1. Mary, Martha and Lazarus offered Jesus friendship, hospitality and a place to escape as they were aware of the demands of his ministry. Who offers such things to those who offer ministry in your church?

2. Mary and Martha were two very different people. What are the values of both the contemplative and active lifestyles in the Christian community?

3. Was Mary's offering of perfume wasteful?
   How do you feel about having beautiful and valuable things in churches? Should they be sold and given to the poor?

4. Why were the religious leaders fearful of Jesus' ability to raise the dead?
   What do his words about being the resurrection and the life mean to you?

Tomb, One Careful, Short-term Occupant.
John 19:38 - 42

If I give a gift I don't expect to receive it back three days later, nor do I normally give away expensive things that I bought for my future, but these have been strange days.

I'd bought my tomb years ago, a bit of an investment and security for the future. It wasn't cheap even when I bought it because it's in a prime position just outside the city walls. I'd never have sold it even to make a profit and I could have made a handsome profit on it, and it certainly wouldn't have crossed my mind to give it away, especially to someone I hardly knew, but that's exactly what I did.

I got caught up in events that seemed to me to be of profound significance; more than just a matter of right or wrong, truth or falsehood. These were events that shook me to the core and got me to question my priorities, beliefs and actions, or rather inactions. Jesus turned my world upside down without, I suspect, ever knowing it.

I'm a member of the Sanhedrin, the Jewish ruling council made up of Pharisees and Sadducees who most of the time don't agree on very much. The one thing they did agree on in recent days was the fate of Jesus. Although for different reasons they were unanimous in their hostility towards him and their certainty that he must be disposed of whatever the cost.

He had been accused of being a lawbreaker, showing little regard for the Sabbath rules, he claimed to have the authority to forgive sins, putting himself on a par with God. Many of the leading religious figureheads felt threatened by his popularity which undermined their own. He was loved, they were merely feared, not even respected. He had certainly built up a huge following among the ordinary people who responded to his direct and accessible teaching and of course his miracles. It was said he had claimed to be the long awaited Messiah and such claims were believed to destabilise the position of our religion, indeed our nation. Our High Priest had already said it was better for one man, Jesus, to die than for the whole nation to be destroyed.

Strangely though, Pilate didn't see him as such a threat, he was somewhat dismissive of the allegations brought against Jesus and tried to release him with a warning. But the religious leaders whipped people up into an irrational frenzy maintaining that Jesus was dangerous, subversive, blasphemous and was undermining the very survival of the Jewish nation. It became increasingly clear they would be satisfied with nothing less than his crucifixion which only Pilate could authorise.

I feel ashamed of myself. I had come to believe in him. I could see his integrity, the way in which his life shone with God's love. I could understand his criticism of our religion with all its pettiness and focusing on peripheral things whilst losing sight of God's love and mercy. I knew he wasn't dangerous, he didn't want to cause an uprising only a spiritual purification of our religious laws and practices. There was nothing in him but pure goodness.

Perhaps he was too good, too close to God for us to accommodate.

I could have spoken out in his defence, I could have denounced the travesty of a trial he underwent but instead I did nothing, I said nothing. I was paralysed by fear. Fear for my reputation, fear for my popularity, fear for my place on the Sanhedrin. There was I immobilised by fear of what after all were fairly inconsequential things whilst he fearlessly accepted his death, the agonizing, humiliating death of crucifixion.

Of course it was too little too late but I determined that he should be afforded the recognition and dignity in death that he had been denied in life. When I heard that he had died I asked Pilate for his body, and helped by Nicodemus I anointed his body, wrapped it in burial cloths and placed it in my tomb. We had to do it quickly because the Sabbath was approaching when no work could be done, but we would return once the Sabbath had ended to give him a more careful burial, or so we thought.

At break of day on the first day of the week when Sabbath was ended rumours were flying around that the tomb was empty, that Jesus had been seen, alive, raised from the dead. In the days that followed, his mother, Mary Magdalene and his disciples met him in various places and attested to the incredible fact that God had raised him from the dead.

What do you do with a tomb in which God raised his son to life? I couldn't even contemplate being buried in such a holy place. I'm on the lookout for another tomb for myself.

I Shared My Son in Law with Him.
Mark 1:16 - 31, Luke 22:54 - 62, John 21: 15 -17

There have been countless jokes and quips about the relationship between married men and their mothers' in law, but in our case it was a relationship made in heaven. Simon was a perfect catch for my daughter, if you'll excuse the pun. Simon was a fisherman on the Sea of Galilee. He and his brother Andrew worked with their father Jonah, and they were in partnership with James and John and their father Zebedee. It was a thriving business, people always wanted to buy fresh fish.

Simon was a strong man, broad and muscular, used to hard work which I admired in a man, but sometimes, no, quite often he spoke without thinking, he was impetuous. To those who didn't know him well he could appear bluff but he had a heart of gold. We were always close. He'd come back to my house and share meals with us, usually bringing some fish, and he'd chat about the day's activities. He was solid, sensible and dependable.

One day he came back to the house as usual and you could have knocked me down with a feather when he told me he was giving up fishing. 'What Simon, have you taken leave of your senses?' I asked him. 'It runs in the family, it's the only job you've ever known, you're good at it and it provides a reliable income. What are you thinking of doing'. Mum he said, it's going to be hard to explain. He said they were fishing on the lake as usual and this teacher, Jesus, told us to leave our nets and follow him, and we did. Well, I couldn't believe what he'd just told me. 'You walked off and decided to follow an itinerant preacher that you'd never met before? Whatever will your poor father think? He'd built up that business and expected to hand it on to you and Andrew. How will you earn a living wandering around the countryside with a penniless preacher?' Simon said he didn't know but he knew it was something he just had to do. There was something compelling about Jesus, his look, his voice, his authority. I knew there was no way of talking Simon out of this, he could be stubborn and rarely changed his mind. I must say I was longing to meet this Jesus to see for myself what made him so special.

I hadn't expected such a dramatic encounter. I was in bed, feeling absolutely awful; I'd never had such a fever. The four fishermen arrived at my house and with them was a man I'd never met before. Was this real or was I delirious and imagining things? This stranger gently reached out and took me by the hand and helped me out of bed. It was remarkable, I can't explain it, but the fever left me immediately. That man was Jesus. Of course now it made perfect sense why Simon and the others left their nets and followed him. I too decided to follow him, to serve him in my own way. I was so grateful for my restoration to health my immediate reaction was to say 'Thank you' in the best way I knew, making a meal for them all and waiting at table on them. From then on I said to Jesus my house was always available to him if he wanted hospitality or just a place to rest. I wanted to think that in some small way I could help him in his work.

I was always eager to hear from Simon where they'd been and what they'd done: what an adventure those uneducated fishermen had embarked on. I was pleased that Jesus recognized the qualities in Simon that I had always so admired. He gave him a new name, Cephas, rock. Like me, Jesus had seen his strength of character and his loyalty.

He clearly had great plans for Simon which unfolded over the coming months and the next three years. All of our lives were transformed in unimaginable ways by the presence and friendship of Jesus. Even when I didn't see Jesus I got regular updates about what he and his disciples had been up to. At first I was amazed when I heard how he'd fed five thousand people with one boy's picnic lunch; transformed huge quantities of water into the finest quality wine; healed paralysed people, lepers, and the blind. After a while I almost began to take it for granted: it was what he did.

Out of all the miracles though one particularly impressed Simon and he never tired of telling this tale. As I've said, Simon was a strong man and a very experienced fisherman. He was used to storms on the lake and knew how to deal with them. He could also read the signs of the weather and knew when not to go out. But he told me of the day that he and the others were absolutely terrified and thought their end had come. They had set off for a day's fishing on the lake when suddenly, out of nowhere, a great storm erupted. The boat was being tossed about like flotsam and was filling with water. Their attempts to bail out were proving futile. They were all panicking, desperately doing things to try to steady the boat and preserve their lives; all of them except Jesus that is. He was asleep, unperturbed and oblivious to the fact that they were caught up in a life threatening situation. Simon said at the time he was angry with Jesus. He said he couldn't believe his apparent lack of concern about their wellbeing. He shouted at Jesus asking if he didn't care that they were perishing. Of course later he regretted his outburst. Apparently Jesus spoke to the roaring waves as if they were a person, addressing them with authority and commanding them to calm down. Amazingly they obeyed him and there was a great calm. Jesus then turned to the disciples and asked them where their faith was and why they doubted him. Of course they felt duly chastened and realised they should have trusted him in all things.

It wasn't just his miracles though, Simon said Jesus' teaching was unlike anything people had heard before. He didn't teach in a bookish way he used illustrations from the things around him, everyday things that ordinary people were familiar with. He asked his hearers questions and engaged in a conversation with them. He told stories which gripped their attention and got them to work out the meaning. His stories turned things upside down, they showed a different view of the world and a fresh set of values where the poor and marginalized were centre stage and the self-important religious leaders were on the periphery. He forgave the sinful and welcomed the outcast; he associated with the most unlikely people, but Simon explained that all of this made him unpopular with respected religious authorities. He kept saying one day there was going to be a show down and he wasn't looking forward to it. He was right; things all came to a head at Passover time.

Jesus and his disciples had all gone up to Jerusalem to observe the festival. I had an instinctive sense of foreboding, I wished they weren't going. I knew they were going to be away from Galilee for a while and I prayed daily for their safety and wellbeing. I heard rumours that Jesus had been arrested and was facing serious charges, I hoped there was no substance to them. It was only when Simon and the others came home that I heard what had happened and by then the whole landscape had changed: Jesus had been arrested, crucified and a few days later raised to life again.

I can't imagine what an emotional rollercoaster it must have been for Simon and the others to live through those days.

As Simon told the story he said that night in the High Priest's courtyard was the lowest point of his life; he was filled with an overwhelming sense of shame and remorse at having said three times that he didn't know Jesus. I tried to tell him that I was sure Jesus would understand and forgive him. Today, Simon has just come and told me that's exactly what happened. Jesus forgave him, gave him a new start and reminded him of his calling. What a restoration and re-affirmation. Jesus once again entrusted his work to Simon, Peter, the rock, telling him to tend his lambs and feed his sheep. Now that he knows without a doubt that Jesus is alive, I think he will more than rise to the challenge. I think he and the others will do amazing things for Jesus. It feels like this is just the beginning of a whole new chapter.